Based on the award-winn

THE ONE O'CLOCK

MIRACLE

Art and activity book

thegoodbook
for children

The One O'Clock Miracle Art and Activity Book
© The Good Book Company 2017

'The Good Book For Children' is an imprint of The Good Book Company Ltd
Tel: 0333 123 0880 International: +44 (0) 208 942 0880   Email: info@thegoodbook.co.uk

North America: www.thegoodbook.com UK: www.thegoodbook.co.uk
Australia: www.thegoodbook.com.au New Zealand: www.thegoodbook.co.nz

Design and illustration by André Parker, based on original illustrations by Catalina Echeverri

ISBN: 9781784982201 Printed in India

Long, long ago there lived
an important man who worked
for the King.
He was sad and
so, so worried.

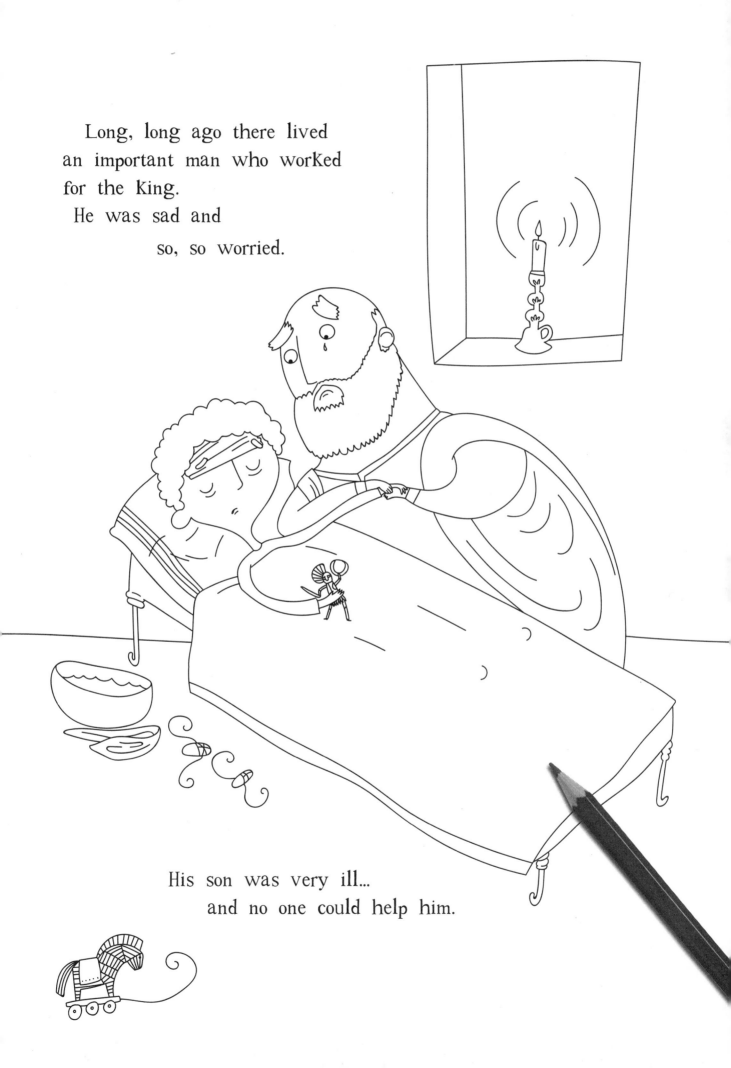

His son was very ill...
and no one could help him.

But then he heard that a man named Jesus was doing the most amazing, wonderful things.

He heard that Jesus was making unwell people well again.

Finish the picture by drawing lots of amazing things that Jesus did!

So the man decided to ask Jesus for help.

A long journey

CAPERNAUM

It was a very long walk –
and uphill all the way!

Sea
of
Galilee

CANA

Can you draw a path
from Capernaum to
Cana? Now decorate
your picture!

Spot the difference

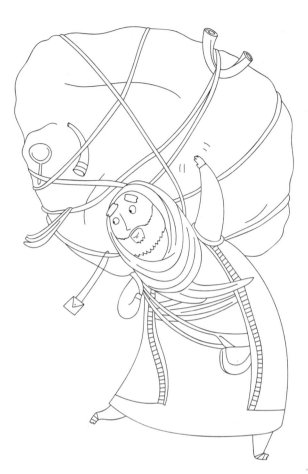

Can you find the 6 differences between these two pictures?

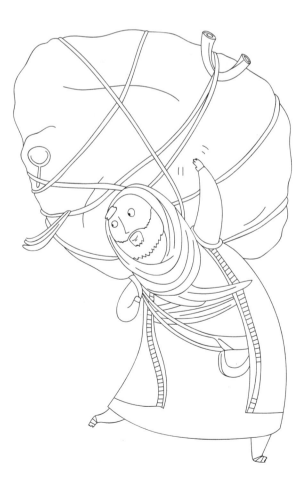

But the man had decided that
he **MUST** see Jesus.

Up the hill, he walked and walked
– and sometimes ran – because he
wanted so badly to see Jesus.

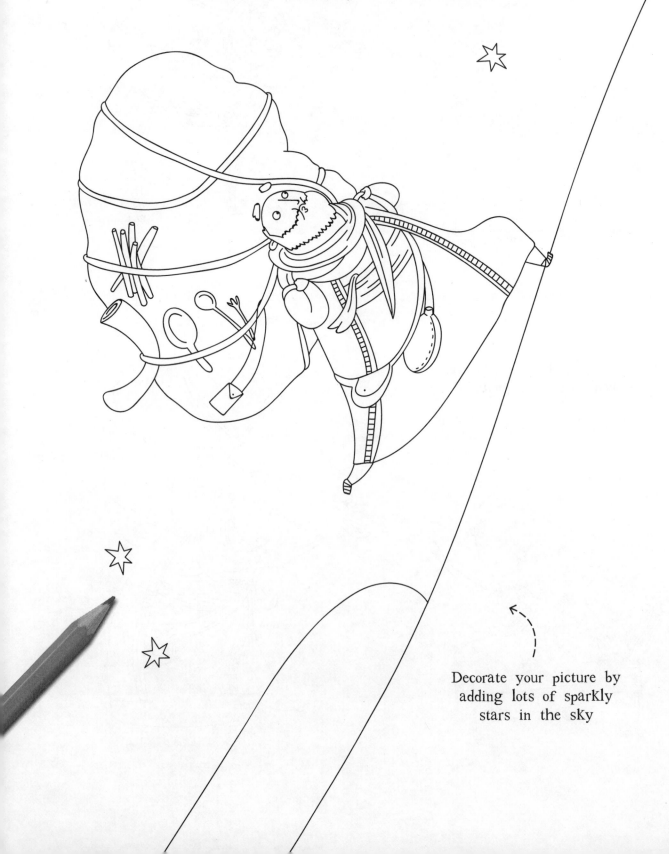

Decorate your picture by
adding lots of sparkly
stars in the sky

Wordsearch

h	K	i	g	b	h	r	g	s	y	s	r	j	h	l
n	a	m	a	z	i	n	g	r	z	e	o	e	a	y
e	K	i	j	u	f	t	r	h	l	r	s	p	d	j
u	c	r	m	a	g	t	e	g	l	K	r	d	n	e
y	a	e	w	e	s	b	n	b	g	a	a	o	a	s
h	n	o	a	n	a	i	r	a	s	l	s	v	K	u
p	a	z	l	a	K	e	l	o	o	r	s	i	g	s
y	o	i	K	b	g	l	i	l	d	y	i	r	c	a
l	K	h	u	n	i	p	e	l	a	K	i	d	l	K
a	l	x	e	h	v	t	t	p	s	h	e	r	u	n
z	j	g	p	p	s	u	f	s	z	t	b	a	h	o
s	i	u	p	r	a	i	c	h	u	f	s	t	f	m
e	t	m	a	n	l	y	r	g	j	t	o	i	i	n
c	o	g	j	t	h	e	l	p	y	u	n	n	t	l
s	g	o	o	d	b	y	e	v	e	x	i	i	f	a

- ☐ man
- ☐ king
- ☐ sad
- ☐ sick
- ☐ son
- ☐ amazing
- ☐ Jesus
- ☐ help
- ☐ Cana
- ☐ uphill
- ☐ walk
- ☐ goodbye

What's the time?

At last, at one o'clock in the
afternoon, the man reached Cana,
the town where Jesus was.

 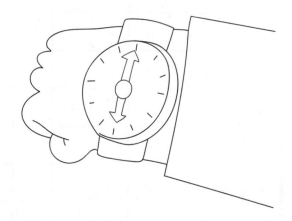

Which of these says
1 o'clock?

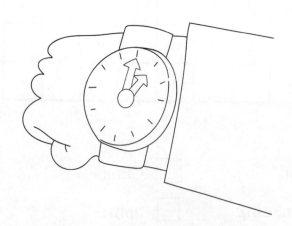 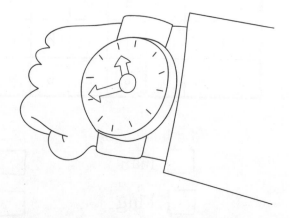

Cana maze

He had walked and walked — and sometimes run — and now, at last, he could see Jesus.

Can you help the man get to Jesus?

"Go," Jesus said.
    But then he added:

The man
BELIEVED
him.

He **TRUSTED**
that what Jesus
said was true.

Wordsearch

h	p	i	d	g	e	y	b	e	l	i	e	v	e	u
m	s	t	a	r	s	b	s	r	z	a	K	e	b	y
a	K	a	j	u	r	t	r	a	b	b	n	v	e	m
g	w	r	r	o	g	a	e	s	r	a	n	d	l	o
m	h	e	t	l	p	b	y	b	i	a	i	o	l	r
a	e	l	i	n	o	e	K	t	d	f	g	d	s	n
r	o	z	c	a	n	n	r	o	t	t	h	d	p	i
v	o	h	i	r	d	e	g	g	t	e	t	i	r	n
l	K	h	u	a	p	p	e	l	e	r	i	s	o	g
a	l	o	r	r	x	t	f	s	i	n	u	h	u	n
z	j	h	f	p	r	j	y	n	x	o	a	s	t	o
s	i	o	p	h	g	y	w	i	h	o	o	r	t	p
j	e	g	u	d	y	i	n	g	n	n	i	c	a	n
t	e	r	a	p	i	d	a	s	h	u	l	i	v	e
m	o	o	n	t	e	y	m	s	o	d	o	r	y	g

☐ journey   ☐ hurry   ☐ dying

☐ night   ☐ morning   ☐ believe

☐ stars   ☐ long   ☐ trust

☐ moon   ☐ afternoon ☐ live

Going home

Can you draw a path for the
man to take?

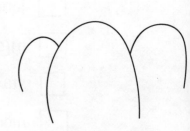

How about
some fish?

Will the path
go through the
mountains?

Draw lots of
trees here.

CAPERNAUM

Down the hill, he walked and walked — and sometimes ran —

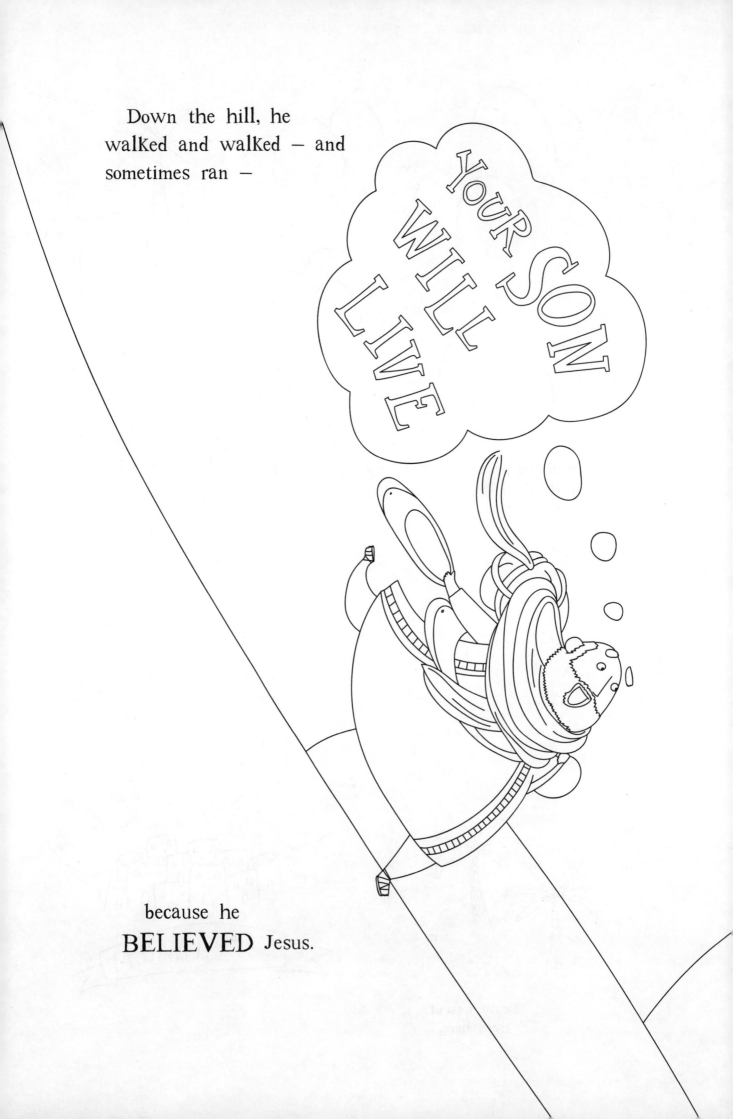

because he **BELIEVED** Jesus.

Who's that?

Then, far away in the distance,
he saw some men.

They must have news, he
thought – but what would it be?

Who's
coming? Can
you draw
them?

"He's alive!"

"Your son is ALIVE! He is WELL AGAIN!"

"WHEN?" the man asked.
"When did he get better?"

"Yesterday. At
ONE O'CLOCK
in the afternoon."

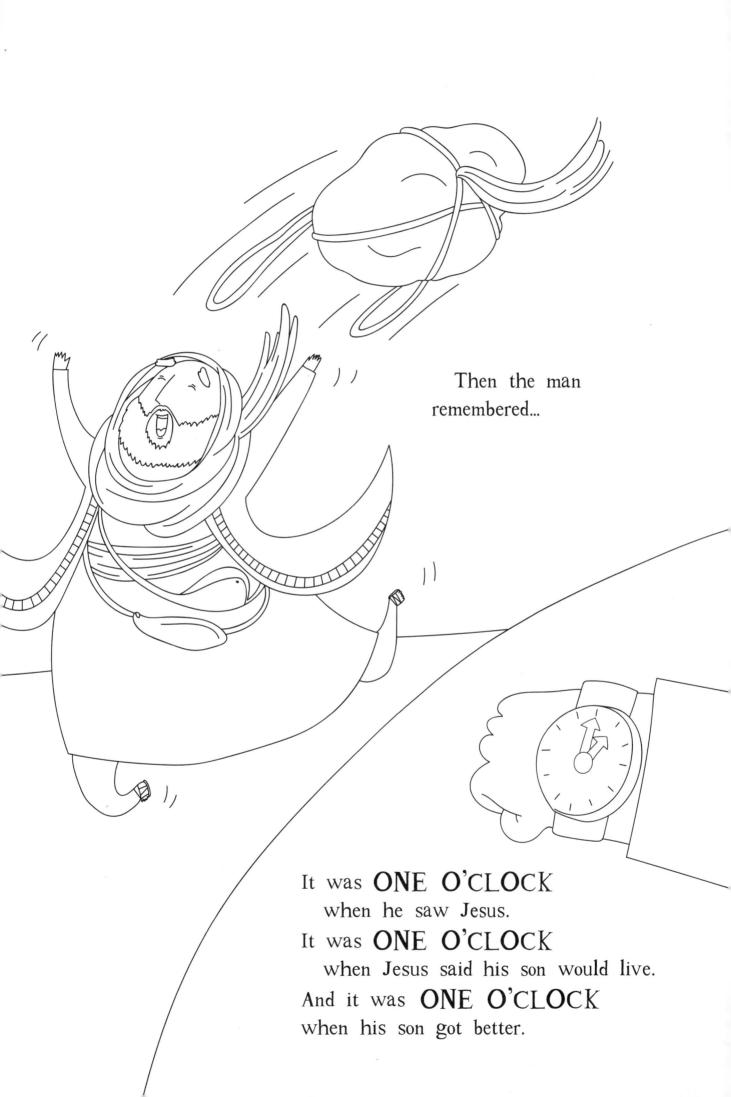

Then the man
remembered...

It was **ONE O'CLOCK**
 when he saw Jesus.
It was **ONE O'CLOCK**
 when Jesus said his son would live.
And it was **ONE O'CLOCK**
 when his son got better.

Jesus didn't need to go
and see the boy.

JESUS

simply...

Decorate this picture so it looks amazing and bright!

— and just like that, the boy was better.
WOW! Only Jesus could do that!

And do you know why? Because **JESUS IS GOD'S SON!**

Welcome home!

Happy and smiling, the man walked
home to see his son again.
Then he told his son and his family
about Jesus.

A happy ending

How does the man feel now?
Put a ✓ next to the right face:

And now that the man's son
was well again,
what could he do?

He could smile and he could laugh,
he could walk and he could run,
and all because of JESUS!

Answers

Spot the difference

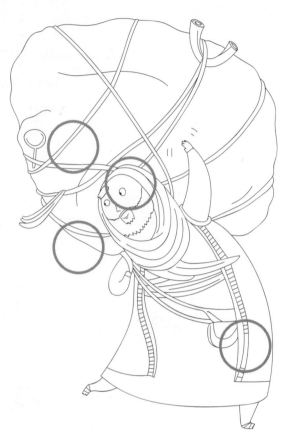

Wordsearch 1

h	K	i	g	b	h	r	g	s	y	s	r	j	h	l
n	a	m	a	z	i	n	g	r	z	e	o	e	a	y
e	K	i	j	u	f	t	r	h	l	r	s	p	d	j
u	c	r	m	a	g	t	e	g	l	K	r	d	n	e
y	a	e	w	e	s	b	n	b	g	a	a	o	a	s
h	n	o	a	n	a	i	r	a	s	l	s	v	K	u
p	a	z	l	a	K	e	l	o	o	r	s	i	g	s
y	o	i	K	b	g	l	i	l	d	y	i	r	c	a
l	K	h	u	n	i	p	e	l	a	K	i	d	l	K
a	l	x	e	h	v	t	t	p	s	h	e	r	u	n
z	j	g	p	p	s	u	f	s	z	t	b	a	h	o
s	i	u	p	r	a	i	c	h	u	f	s	t	f	m
e	t	m	a	n	l	y	r	g	j	t	o	i	i	n
c	o	g	j	t	h	e	l	p	y	u	n	n	t	l
s	g	o	o	d	b	y	e	v	e	x	i	s	f	a

What's the time?

Cana maze

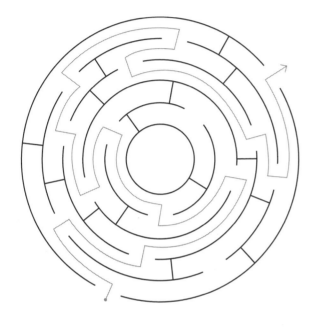

Wordsearch 2

h	p	i	d	g	e	y	b	e	l	i	e	v	e	u
m	s	t	a	r	s	b	s	r	z	a	K	e	b	y
a	k	a	j	u	r	t	r	a	b	b	n	v	e	m
g	w	r	r	o	g	a	e	s	r	a	n	d	l	o
m	h	e	t	l	p	b	y	b	i	a	i	o	l	r
a	e	l	i	n	o	e	K	t	d	f	g	d	s	n
r	o	z	c	a	n	n	r	o	t	t	h	d	p	i
v	o	h	i	r	d	e	g	g	t	e	t	i	r	n
l	k	h	u	a	p	p	e	l	e	r	i	s	o	g
a	l	o	r	r	x	t	f	s	i	n	u	h	u	n
z	j	h	f	p	r	j	y	n	x	o	a	s	t	o
s	i	o	p	h	g	y	w	i	h	o	o	r	t	p
j	e	g	u	d	y	i	n	g	n	n	i	c	a	n
t	e	r	a	p	i	d	a	s	h	u	l	i	v	e
m	o	o	n	t	e	y	m	s	o	d	o	r	y	g

A happy ending

Now read the book!

If you enjoyed this activity book, read the full
story in 'The One O'Clock Miracle.'

Other books available in the award-winning 'Tales that Tell the Truth' series:

Meet God's Rescuing King in 'The Christmas Promise'

Find out the story of the whole Bible in 'The Garden, the Curtain and the Cross'

Discover who Jesus really is in 'The Storm That Stopped'

All available here

www.thegoodbook.com
www.thegoodbook.co.uk